Backpacking Vancouver Island 101

Plan Your Travel, Pack the Right Gear, Safely Explore Nature, and Confidently Take on an Epic Hiking Adventure

Dominique Levesque

Copyright © 2024 by Dominique Levesque

All rights reserved.

No portion of this book may be reproduced in any form without written permission from the publisher or author, except as permitted by U.S. copyright law.

This publication is designed to provide accurate and authoritative information in regard to the subject matter covered. It is sold with the understanding that neither the author nor the publisher is engaged in rendering legal, investment, accounting or other professional services. While the publisher and author have used their best efforts in preparing this book, they make no representations or warranties with respect to the accuracy or completeness of the contents of this book and specifically disclaim any implied warranties of merchantability or fitness for a particular purpose. No warranty may be created or extended by sales representatives or written sales materials. The advice and strategies contained herein may not be suitable for your situation. You should consult with a professional when appropriate. Neither the publisher nor the author shall be liable for any loss of profit or any other commercial damages, including but not limited to special, incidental, consequential, personal, or other damages.

Book Cover by Oleksiy Khmelov

Book Cover Photo Credit: Wade Jordan Wade

1st edition 2024

Contents

Dedication	IV
1. Introduction	1
2. Who Should Go on a Multi-Day Hike?	3
3. About the Land	7
4. Setting the Scene and What to Expect	11
5. Safety	21
6. Reading Tide Tables and Planning a Safe Passage	27
7. Planning Your Trip in 12 Easy Steps	33
8. What to Pack	47
9. How to Pack	62
10. Summary of Hikes, Planning Timeline, and Packing Checklist	66
11. Conclusion	71
Resources and References	72

I'm dedicating this guidebook to my late love, Drew.

You wore your leather, city backpack on our first day hike and, less than one year later, you eagerly conquered your first multi-day hike. Thank you for your openness and enthusiasm to adventure with me.

I'd comb an eternity's worth of beaches to find your bones amongst the stones that catch my tears.

Chapter One

Introduction

Hello and welcome to your Vancouver Island backpacking guidebook! My name is Dominique and I am super keen on helping you prepare for your backpacking adventure on the beautiful coast of Vancouver Island, BC, Canada.

Preparing for a multi-day hike can be intimidating and overwhelming. You may be asking yourself: What do I need to bring? How do I map out my hike? What's a tide chart and why do I care about it? What do I do if I run into a bear? And you might be questioning whether you are even the type of person who should be going on a backpacking trip.

There are many things to consider when you go off into the wild for a few days. My goal is to give you enough information that you can make informed decisions about your hike, but not enough information to spoil your discovery of the unknown. With this guidebook in your hands and its checklists at your fingertips, you will know exactly what to do, why you're doing it, and when to do it. I'm going to help you prepare so that you feel empowered and unstoppably confident to take on your outdoor adventure of a lifetime!

Who am I to be helping you navigate this trip? I'm an outdoor adventure enthusiast who has gone on countless backcountry excursions. I like to ski off-piste, I go outdoor rock climbing, and I enjoy snowshoeing in the mountains. More importantly, I have successfully completed several week-long hikes on Vancouver Island (successful = no injury or rescue required). I have an organized method of preparing for and executing a multi-day hike that significantly reduces my stress about the trip and gets me fired up to tackle the trail. And I'm excited to share my insights with you so that you can experience the magnificence of these remote locations while you challenge yourself physically and mentally.

This guidebook is intended to inform you about some of Vancouver Island's coastal hikes. However, most of this information can be applied to hikes all over the world. I won't talk about the poisonous spiders in the Grand Canyon, the oxygen levels up in the higher mountains, or tell you how to build a snow fort, so please research the area in which you'd like to hike to learn more about how to prepare for the elements you'll be facing. Knowledge is power – it keeps you prepared, safe, and alive.

Chapter Two

Who Should Go on a Multi-Day Hike?

Multi-day hikes are there for (almost) anyone to tackle and enjoy. Having the right attitude, proper physical conditioning, and some backcountry and safety knowledge is essential in ensuring your trip is successful and enjoyable.

Multi-day hikes are tough – physically and mentally – and require strength and stamina. Having a positive mindset despite facing challenges is mandatory and knowing what you're getting into goes a long way in preparing yourself mentally for this incredible physical feat. Not only are you hiking dense rainforest and miles of beaches for 5-12 hours per day, but you are also carrying a 30-50-pound pack that contains your camp, your kitchen, your gear, your clothes, your first aid kit, and the food you will need for the duration of your trip. You will fall, you will get blisters, and you will get a sunburn. You will not sleep well. You will get dirty, feel exhausted, be hungry, and you will miss running water, electricity, and the many comforts of home. So, why even take on a multi-day hike?

The West Coast Trail (WCT) was my very first thru-hike. Finishing this 75-kilometre (47-mile) hike was the most exhilarating, most energizing, and the most empowering challenge I have ever conquered. Something magical happens during a longer backpacking trip that you don't experience on shorter, 2-3-day hikes. Completely cut-off from civilization, I truly disconnected from my daily life and I focused on the beauty and the power of nature and surrounding wilderness, the thrill of exploring new terrain, and the meaningful connections I made with my hike-mates through our shared experience. When you spend a week braving nature and its elements, living without the comforts of home, and relying solely on yourself and your crew, you finish the hike energized and in a state of elated bliss and euphoria, ready to do it all over again. ...after a well-deserved (and needed!) shower and a burger, of course! So, if you want to disconnect, escape the city, and explore nature in places where few have gone before, multi-day hiking might be for you.

You should complete at least one overnight hike before attempting a multi-day hike. Of course, more experience is always better. I completed two separate overnight hikes prior to my first thru-hike, where I familiarized myself with my gear by hiking, setting up camp, building a fire, cooking and cleaning, and tearing down camp the next morning. Although I am an avid hiker, I wanted to ensure I was also physically capable of hauling a heavy pack up and down the many (over 100!) ladders on the WCT, so I trained during the months leading up to the hike. I went on one hike per week and, as I got more fit, I added weight to my backpack to simulate the conditions I'd be faced with on the trail. With this training strategy, I found that I was more than prepared to tackle the WCT and its difficult terrain.

Those who have pre-existing injuries should consult with their health care specialists before attempting a thru-hike. These trips are not for small children. In fact, the WCT does not allow children under 6 to participate. Dogs are not typically allowed on the trail, either. Finally, having a flexible schedule is important as you might need extra time to finish the hike, especially if you run into bad weather. My crew and I had planned to complete the WCT in 6 days but because of heavy rains and my hiking partner's ultra heavy backpack (64 lbs!

Or, to quote my humorous hike mate Graig, "64, baby!"), we ended up needing 7 days. It's a good thing we packed extra food!

Chapter Three

About the Land

PRESERVING AND PROTECTING
The trails along Vancouver Island's coast are steeped in history and offer an immersive journey through rugged landscapes and rich culture. These trails occupy diverse terrain, including lush temperate rainforests, dramatic cliffs, and pristine beaches. Respect for the land and its cultural significance is essential as many trails pass through territories that have been inhabited by First Nations since time immemorial.

The First Nations Guardians work with Parks Canada to protect and preserve the natural and cultural history of the land. Their collaboration demonstrates the nations' philosophy of "hish uk tsa wak," meaning "all is one," and "lisaak," meaning "respect." They encourage visitors to understand this philosophy by behaving respectfully and by sharing their culture and history. Doing so will ensure a safe and rewarding experience for hikers and contribute to a healthy ecosystem for all to appreciate and enjoy, now and going forward.

MY FAVOURITE TRAILS ON VANCOUVER ISLAND
The coast of Vancouver Island is home to several trails, including the world-famous West Coast Trail (WCT). Other noteworthy trails are the Nootka Trail, the North Coast & Cape Scott Trail, and the Tatchu Peninsula Trail. Due

to their remote location, preparing for these trails demands careful planning and months of preparation (see Chapter 7 for the 12 steps involved in planning for these hikes). These four trails are summarized in the table in Chapter 10; here is an overview of each.

West Coast Trail. Originally a path used by the Nuu-chah-nulth First Nations people for trade and travel, this trail later became a vital route for shipwreck survivors during the late 19th and early 20th centuries as European settlers arrived and maritime traffic increased.

Today, the WCT is a legendary 75-kilometre (47-mile) hiking route filled with history and natural beauty. This trail is one of the world's premier wilderness treks and sees over 7,500 hikers per season. MapQuest lists the WCT as one of the ten toughest and most dangerous treks in the world, boasting challenging terrain that includes ladders, cable cars, and tide-dependent sections. Most people hike this trail in 5-8 days. We hiked the WCT in 7 days (without a rest day – rookie mistake). I would hike the WCT again but, this time, in 8 days, and I'd include a rest day in the middle. Each multi-day hike we've completed since the WCT has included a rest day and we've had no regrets; rest days are a game changer, really.

Nootka Trail. The Nootka Trail is a shorter (36 km/ 22 miles), easier version of the WCT and only about 500 hikers hike this trail per year. The majority of the hike is along the beach and there are fewer tidal obstacles to plan for. Most people take 4-6 days to hike this trail. We took 7 days, which included a rest day at Calvin Falls (I highly recommend a rest day here). Part of the trail borders on private property so stay on the trail and respect the locals' privacy. The south end of the trail is in Yuquot, on the traditional lands of the Mowachaht and Muchalaht First Nations. Take in the history and culture by visiting the church and by speaking to Darrell, the son of the chief.

Totem pole inside the church on Nootka Island

The North Coast & Cape Scott Trail. These two trails combine for a hike of 58 km/ 36 miles. The North Coast Trail section is even more remote and rugged than the WCT, thus is deemed by some as more difficult. The Cape Scott portion of the trail is in a national park and is easy hiking. Most complete this combined hike in 5-7 days.

Tatchu Peninsula Trail. The Tatchu Trail is an out-and-back trail (64 km/ 40 miles return) and takes 5-7 days to complete. You can hike this trail one-way, but the logistics of transportation to and from the trailheads are a little more complicated. The Tatchu Trail sees even fewer people per season than the Nootka and is rougher, although it has some of the most pristine sandy beaches in BC. Interestingly, a portion of the beach trek is magma rock from the Jurassic era and has many embedded fossils to marvel at. A rest day at Rugged Point is recommended.

At the time of writing this guidebook, I am preparing to hike the North Coast & Cape Scott Trail, having completed the other three hikes in previous years. I invite you to join me as we prepare for our great outdoor adventure!

Chapter Four

Setting the Scene and What to Expect

Before getting into logistics and packing, let's first talk a little more about what you're getting yourself into. Knowing what to expect on the trail will help you understand how to best prepare for it, which will reduce your anxiety about the trip, keep you safe, and make your trip more enjoyable.

You are backpacking the coastal rainforest on an island at the edge of the world. And this land is wild. There is no electricity, no cell signal; there are no houses, no stores, and barely any people. When you're in the forest, all you see is forest, and when on the beach, all you see is the endless, open ocean and miles of beach in either direction. The scene is glorious and like that of a postcard, but there are elements that may pose dangers and thus merit mention.

THE BEACH

Although breathtakingly beautiful, the beaches are not always sandy and can be tricky to walk on. Some beaches are covered in pebbles and your feet sink at every step, making the trek a little more difficult. Other beaches are covered in fist-sized rocks or larger stones you can hop across, boulders you need to scramble (use your hands), logs, lava rock, or even kelp, which is very slippery, slimy, and very stinky (avoid falling here!). When trekking at low tide, you can hike along the ocean floor, which is spectacular, but can be slippery.

* GAME CHANGER * Invest in a pair of gaiters – a piece of cloth, typically a little rigid and waterproof, that wraps around your shin from your ankle to your knee and clips to your shoe. Gaiters protect your shins against bumps and scrapes and keep you clean from the mud, and also prevent sand, pebbles, twigs, and mud from going into your shoes.

GOOD TO KNOW! While hiking along the beaches, be on the lookout for whales – humpbacks, gray whales, and orcas – as well as seals, sea lions, and otters. You might even come across bones or a whale skeleton you can investigate.

My hiking crew and me, marvelling at whale bones along the coast of Nootka Island. From left to right: Jré, Dylan, Graig, Kyle, Drew, me, Abra, and Wade.

THE FOREST

The forest sections can be quite gnarly as you are trekking through dense, old-growth rainforest. You have to navigate large mud puddles by stepping on random roots and logs; the boardwalks (if there) are in dire shape; ropes and steep ladders help you climb uphill, but rungs are often missing or worn out; cable cars carry you across bodies of water; and, sometimes, the trail is on the edge of a cliff so you have to be extra careful with your footing.

Wade and me, navigating mud puddles and weathered boardwalks along the WCT

Wade is thrilled to soar above the river in a cable car on the WCT

RIVERS, CREEKS, AND WADING

Some sections require that you wade across a river. Before crossing, unclip your backpack waist and chest straps; if you fall into the water you will have to remove your pack quickly. I remove my gaiters and wear lightweight water shoes for these crossings to keep my hiking boots dry. Sandals are not recommended as they can slip off with the current. The current can be quite strong even in shin-deep water and the rock bed underfoot is slippery, so use your poles and shuffle your feet as you move. Face upstream for better balance and travel at an angle with the current instead of fighting against it (ie., allow yourself to slip downstream diagonally). You can also cross as a group, side by side, linking arms for more stability.

CAUTION! If you fall in the water, remove your pack, stay on your back, point your feet downstream, and swim to shore or calmer water.

Drew and me, wading across a creek on Nootka Island as the tide comes in

WEATHER

You are hiking the coastal rainforest along the pacific ocean, so expect all types of weather: heavy winds, tidal waves, rain, fog, mist, clouds, and sunshine. Due to the potential for rapidly changing weather, it's essential to bring adequate gear (rain jacket and rain pants, tarp, etc). Although rare, tsunamis are a possible occurrence:

CAUTION! If you feel the ground shake and you see the ocean water flooding or receding from the beach, get to higher ground and as far inland as you can. Some trails (like the WCT) will have an evacuation route you can follow in the event of a tsunami.

THE TIDES

Some spots along the shoreline are impassable at high tide, meaning your path is under water and impossible to hike through. There will either be a forest bypass route you can take instead, or not and you will have to wait until the water recedes before you can cross that section. Alternatively (and better still), you can consult a tide table when planning your route so that you cross these spots during low-mid tide, when the beach is exposed and passable by foot. This latter option is often preferable as forest hiking can take longer than hiking along the beach, and you won't be forced to wait hours for the next low tide before continuing your journey (which sometimes isn't until the next day). See Chapter 6 for details on tide tables and how to use them.

FACILITIES

Showers. Forget showering and forget about running water and plumbing because there is none. It feels weird at first but you quickly become accustomed to being "camp clean." Bathe in the ocean, if needed, and use biodegradable soap, if needed. Do not bathe in fresh water to avoid contaminating it. I'm not a fan of cold water so I like to use wipes. After a day of hiking, we get to camp, set up our tent, and before I change into dry clothes I give myself a sponge bath and feel squeaky clean.

Toilets. Some hiking trails have outhouses at their campsites, some don't. Either way, pack at least one trowel for the group in case nature calls mid-hike and you are not near an outhouse. Make sure you also pack toilet paper and hand sanitizer and/ or antiseptic wipes.

Bathroom breaks. When nature calls and there are no outhouses nearby, you'll need to practice "leave no trace" principles. You can go below the high tide line or into the forest for this moment, but make sure you are at least 200 feet (60 meters; about 70 big steps) from a trail, a campsite, or from a fresh water source. Dig a "cathole" in the ground, about 6-8 inches deep, do your thing, and bury your waste after. You can bury your toilet paper if it's not bleached and biodegradable; you can also bring it to the next outhouse or carry it out with you (some folks triple bag their waste to eliminate odor). Pack out feminine hygiene products.

Food storage. Never store food in your tent or anything else aromatic that could attract animals. Make sure you empty your entire backpack and every pocket in which you stored snacks.

PRO TIP: Use yesterday's empty ziplock bags for today's trash to prevent leakage and crumbs from going into your backpack. I try not to keep empty wrappers free in my backpack to reduce the chance of food scraps attracting animals.

Some trails have food caches (aka bear cache – a large metal box in which to store your food, trash, toiletries, and other aromatics) at every campsite. Where there are no food caches, you will need to hang your aromatics from a tree in what's called a "bear bag," which is just a term for your bag of food/ aromatics. I highly recommend you store your food in a dry bag so that it doesn't get soaked if it rains overnight.

To hang a bear bag, you will need rope (about 40 ft), a locking carabiner, a weighted sac, a branch or stake, and a dry bag that holds your food, trash, and other aromatics. The most popular and effective way of hanging a bear bag is called the PCT (Pacific Coast Trail) method; here is a website with complete instructions on how to do so https://theultimatehang.com/2013/03/19/hanging-a-bear-bag-the-pct-method/.

Where you hang your bear bag is equally important to *how* you hang it. Do not hang your bear bag near your tent; it should be at least 200 feet away and downwind from your tent. Here is a diagram to help you visualize your camp and where your tent, bear bag, and kitchen should be situated relative to one another:

The "Bear"-muda Triangle

Bear Bag — 6 ft down, 2 ft high, 6 ft away — 200 feet — WIND — 200 feet — Sleeping Area — 200 feet — Kitchen area

©2013 Derek Hansen TheUltimateHang.com

BACKCOUNTRY ETIQUETTE & ENVIRONMENTAL STEWARDSHIP

"Leave No Trace" is an American organization with a global reach that focuses on education as the most effective solution to land and wildlife protection. The seven principles of Leave No Trace outline how to treat nature, wildlife, and your fellow hikers, and are often referred to when guiding newcomers to the backcountry.

The 7 Principles of Leave No Trace:

1. Plan ahead and prepare. Know the conditions for the area you are visiting and prepare for extreme weather, hazards, and emergencies;

2. Travel and camp on durable surfaces. Forest environment is sensitive to damage so stick to trails and campsites and use pre-existing fire pits;

3. Dispose of waste properly. Yes, even your orange peel. First, if everyone discarded their orange peels, the forest would soon turn into a com-

post, and it would smell like one. Second, the smell attracts animals. So, if you pack it in, pack it out;

4. Leave what you find. Taking natural artifacts is forbidden;

5. Minimize campfire impacts. Small fires are permitted on the beach below the high tide line, never in the forest;

6. Respect and protect wildlife, from encounters to storing your food and trash properly;

7. Be considerate of others. Yield to other hikers and let nature's sounds prevail by minimizing loud voices and noises.

Follow these principles to make sure you are taking care of each other, wildlife, and the land you are exploring. For more information, please visit https://lnt.org/why/7-principles/.

EXITS

Once on these trails, you are fully committed. Only the WCT has one exit halfway through the hike, at Nitinat. The Nootka, Tatchu, and North Coast & Cape Scott Trails have no exit points besides the trailheads.

Chapter Five

Safety

Many potential dangers exist along your journey, from drinking contaminated water, falling off a ladder and getting hurt, getting lost, and encountering wildlife. While most dangers can be mitigated by paying attention to your footing and carefully planning your route, you may nevertheless find yourself in a situation that compromises your safety or requires medical care. In these situations, remember to stay calm and breathe.

WATER

Never drink salt water unless you desalinate it first, which involves boiling it and collecting the vapour (fresh water). The trails I mention in this guidebook provide plenty of fresh water sources such as rivers and creeks, but you need to filter/ purify it first, even though the water might look clean and fresh. The consequence of not filtering/ purifying your water can be catastrophic; you might become very ill and require a rescue.

You can boil your water, which will kill any disease-causing germs; however, this method requires you to have your stove set up and some time. Water filters physically strain out protozoan cysts such as Cryptosporidium and Giardia lamblia as well as bacteria such as E. coli, Salmonella, Campylobacter and Shigella. Water purifiers use chemicals or ultraviolet (UV) light to kill these cysts and bacteria as well as viruses, which are too small to be strained by most filters. These and other filtration and purification systems worth considering can be read about and compared here: https://www.rei.com/learn/expert-advice/water-treatment-backcountry.html.

GETTING LOST & SURVIVAL

If you get lost. Stay calm and stay as visible as possible. You may be able to backtrack to a known location, but do not wander aimlessly. Follow the trail if there is one; avoid taking shortcuts. Mark your trek by piling rocks or logs on the ground in the shape of an arrow that points in the direction you're travelling. These markers are helpful if you need to back up and they also help rescuers. If you can't find a known territory, find a safe place to spend the night and do so while there is still daylight. Once you find a spot to spend the night, stay put; it's more difficult for searchers to find a moving target.

Building an emergency shelter. You can find shelter in a cave, under a fallen tree, or under dense, overhanging branches. Alternatively, you can create a shelter or a slanted roof using an emergency blanket, a tarp, or a garbage bag supported by sticks, your hiking poles, or some paracord. Face the shelter away from the wind; close the opposite end and face the open end toward a reflecting surface such as a large rock or a cliff. A fire between your shelter and the reflecting surface will heat the shelter. Conserving your body heat is critical for survival, so you want to stay as dry as possible. Pile up dry material inside the shelter to insulate yourself from the cold ground.

Building a fire. To build a fire, gather three types of material: tinder (dead grass, old pine needles, paperlike bark), kindling (dry twigs, branches), and fuel (larger pieces of dry wood, driftwood). Build a pyramid of tinder on dry ground. Next, arrange your kindling in a loose pyramid over the tinder. Set a flame to the tinder. Once the kindling catches fire and is fully involved, add progressively larger pieces of fuel. Keep your material loose to ensure airflow. Save on fuel by keeping your fire small; a small fire will keep you just as warm as a larger one if you sit close to it.

Signalling for help. Smoky fires by day and bright fires by night are effective signals. Adding wet logs to your fire will make it smoky. Three fires set in the shape of an equilateral triangle are a universal call for help. Three whistle blows are also a recognized call for help. You can also use a mirror to signal for help by reflecting sunlight toward the target. Reflected light can be seen for many miles, even on cloudy days.

FIRST AID

Cuts. First, stop the bleeding by applying pressure and elevating the site higher than your heart. Prevent infection by washing the site with clean water. For wounds that are less than half an inch wide, use strips of tape to close the cut and cover the site with ointment, sterile gauze, and tape. For larger wounds, cover with sterile gauze and tape and see a doctor.

Blisters. If intact, wash the site and slice the blister open with a sterilized knife. Let it drain. Protect the skin by applying ointment to the site and creating a foam "doughnut" around the site with moleskin. Cover with tape to keep the ointment and padding in place.

Broken bones. A broken bone will require a splint. Start with padding the area with extra clothing or anything soft. Make sure to not interfere with normal blood circulation. Then, attach something rigid outside the padding to immobilize the joints or bones above and below the break. For example, if you break an ankle, the splint should immobilize the foot and lower leg. Attach the rigid support with whatever you have on hand (elastics, paracord, etc). If you're able to walk out, do so, or set yourself up to wait for a rescue.

WILDLIFE ENCOUNTERS

Vancouver Island is home to black bears, cougars, and wolves. If you don't encounter them on your trek, you will surely see signs of them such as prints and scat. Predators are more likely to stay away from hikers when in a larger group (4 people or more). Speak loudly or sing when hiking to make yourself known to wildlife. Never approach or feed wild animals. If you encounter a predator, do not turn away, do not run, and do not scream, as these behaviors signal to the animal that you are prey and might trigger an attack. Instead, back away slowly, avoid eye contact, and talk to the animal in a calm voice. Make sure the animal has a clear avenue of escape.

Although attacks are very rare, it is useful to know how to handle such a confrontation.

Black bears. Black bears might stand on their hind legs out of curiosity to get a better look and smell; this behavior does not signal aggression. If, however, a black bear woofs aggressively, turns to its side to show you its size, or charges at you, make yourself big by raising your arms or putting your pack above your head and speak louder. If you're in a group, stay close together to appear larger. If it attacks, fight it off by striking its eyes or nose with rocks, sticks, or your hiking poles, or use bear spray; black bears will usually retreat from a counterattack.

Of my countless outback experiences, I have only seen a black bear on the trail once. It was maybe 130 feet (40 meters) away and it was not interested in us at all. We stopped when we saw it; the bear noticed us but we slowly backed away and it carried on doing its thing. We waited until it was out of sight before continuing on our path.

Cougars. If a cougar takes interest in you or follows you, act as though you are the threat and not the prey. Face it; do not look away and keep the cougar in front of you. Make yourself look big, show your teeth, and make noise. Arm yourself with rocks, sticks, or your hiking poles. If a cougar attacks, fight back and strike its eyes, nose, and ears. Make sure the cougar leaves the area first.

When I hiked the WCT, we ended up hiking in the dark one evening (not recommended; we had gotten lost). When we finally arrived at the river near our campsite, my two crewmates were filling our cantines while I scanned the area. It was pitch black outside and my headlamp would only shine light so far, beyond which was total darkness (trippy!). To my left, about 130 feet (40 meters) away, I saw a pair of glowing, green cat eyes looking right back at me. I immediately grabbed my whistle (which is built into my backpack's chest strap), sounded a few blows, and the animal bolted away immediately. Phew! Again, very rarely do predators attack humans.

Cougar paw prints along the sandy beach on the WCT

Wolves. Wolves do not typically attack human adults. If one approaches you, make yourself larger and shout at the wolf in an aggressive voice and throw objects at it.

The takeaway here is that these animals are more cautiously curious about us than they are hungry for us. If you come across one, stay calm, give it space, and don't give it any reason to fear you or challenge you.

Chapter Six

Reading Tide Tables and Planning a Safe Passage

WHAT IS A TIDE TABLE AND WHY DO I NEED ONE?
There are numerous tidal obstacles along the coast, meaning as the tide comes in and the water gets higher, a portion of the trail goes under water and is no longer passable by foot. In order to hike these sections safely, the water must be below a certain height (ie, low-mid tide). Your map will indicate specific areas along the trail where a safe passage must be timed with a certain tide height (eg. "passable at tides below 7 ft/ 2.1 m"). In order to know what time(s) low tide will occur during the day, we need to consult a tide table.

A tide table shows the hourly predictions (times of the day) for tide height for a given geographical location or "station." Refer to the table in Chapter 10 to know which station to look up for your hike.

Let's use an example to first walk through where to find a tide table and how to read it, and then let's go over how to calculate the timing of your hike so that you arrive at this tidal obstacle before it is covered in water and impassable.

WHERE DO I GET A TIDE TABLE?

In this example, we are hiking the West Coast Trail, so the tidal station to lookup is Tofino (station 08615). To get the tide table for the Tofino station:

1. Go to https://www.tides.gc.ca/en/stations/08615. If hiking a different trail, enter the corresponding 5-digit number or select the appropriate station from the list in the "Select Station" drop-down;

2. The timezone should be set to PDT (Pacific Daylight Time; UTC-7);

3. Select your start date (the output will give you data for the week, starting on that day);

4. Select units of measurement (meters or feet);

5. Click Submit.

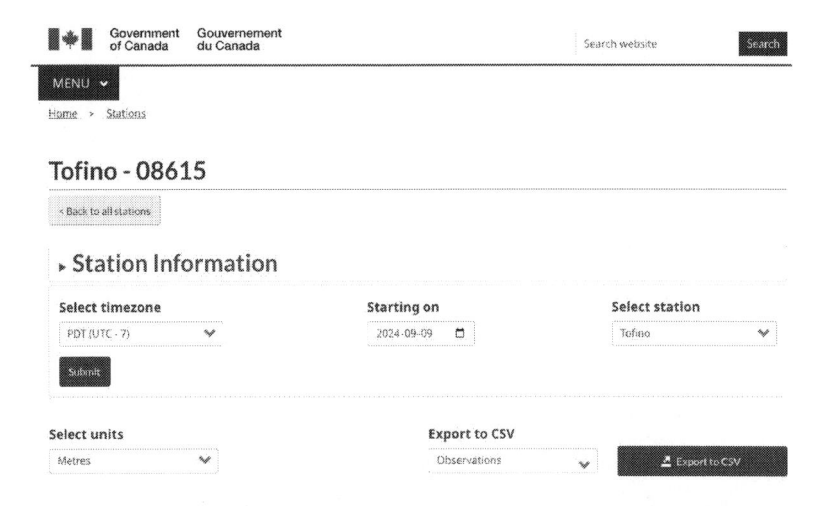

You'll notice the information is presented in chart and table format. We want to scroll to the bottom of the page to a table that displays the hourly height predictions for each day of the week you specified. Here, we are looking at the hourly predictions for the week of August 14-20, 2024.

Hourly Predictions (m)

Event Date	00	01	02	03	04	05	06	07	08	09	10	11	12	13	14	15	16	17	18	19	20	21	22	23
2024-08-14		1.3	1.1	1.1	1.2	1.4	1.6	1.9	2.2	2.3	2.3	2.3	2.2	2	2	2	2.1	2.3	2.6	2.9	3	3	2.8	2.5
2024-08-15	2.1	1.6	1.2	1	0.9	1	1.2	1.5	1.9	2.2	2.4	2.5	2.4	2.3	2.1	2	2.1	2.3	2.6	2.9	3.1	3.1	2.9	
2024-08-16	2.5	2.1	1.5	1.1	0.8	0.7	0.8	1.1	1.5	1.9	2.3	2.6	2.7	2.5	2.3	2.1	1.9	1.9	2	2.3	2.6	3	3.2	3.3
2024-08-17	3	2.6	2	1.4	0.9	0.6	0.5	0.6	1	1.5	2.1	2.5	2.8	2.8	2.6	2.3	1.9	1.7	1.7	1.9	2.2	2.7	3.1	3.4
2024-08-18	3.4	3.1	2.6	1.9	1.2	0.7	0.3	0.3	0.6	1.1	1.7	2.3	2.8	3	2.9	2.5	2.1	1.7	1.5	1.5	1.7	2.2	2.8	3.3
2024-08-19	3.6	3.5	3.2	2.5	1.7	1	0.5	0.2	0.3	0.6	1.3	2	2.7	3.1	3.2	2.9	2.4	1.9	1.5	1.2	1.3	1.6	2.2	2.8
2024-08-20	3.4	3.7	3.6	3.1	2.3	1.5	0.8	0.3	0.1	0.4	0.9	1.6	2.4	3	3.4	3.3	2.8	2.2	1.6	1.2	1	1.1	1.6	2.2
2024-08-21	2.9																							

HOW DO I READ A TIDE TABLE?

If we look at the first day, August 14, we see that the tide is going out (the water height decreases) from 0100 until 0200. Then, from 0300 until 0900, the tide switches directions and comes in, and the tide height increases. You'll notice that there are usually 2 high tides and 2 low tides per day, and the tide heights are different from day to day, so it's very important to look at the correct date when planning your hike.

Now that we know what the tide is doing (coming in or going out) and when, let's go over how to calculate the timing of your hike so that you arrive at those tidal obstacles before the water is too high and the trail becomes impassable.

TIMING YOUR HIKE TO AVOID TIDAL OBSTACLES

Taking a section of the West Coast Trail map as an example, let's go over how to time your hike in 5 easy steps.

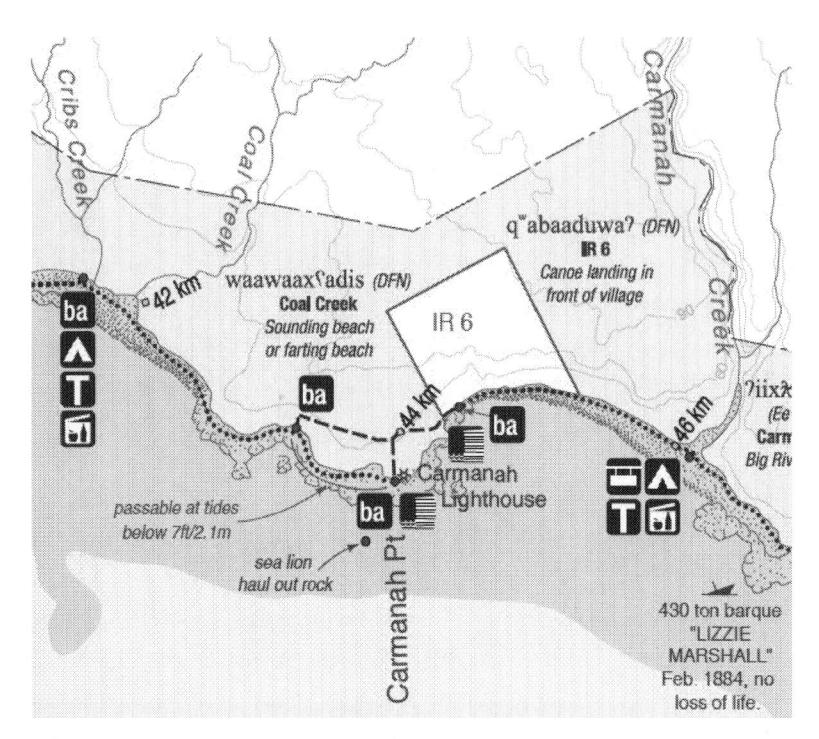

1. Where are you starting from? First, we look at our starting point on the map, which might be the trailhead or a campsite. In this example, we are starting from the campsite at Cribs Creek (at about km 41.5; left hand side of map) and we are heading toward Carmanah Creek (km 46; right hand side of map).

2. Where is the tidal obstacle? The tidal obstacle is roughly between km 43.5 and km 44.

3. What is the distance from our starting point to the tidal obstacle? Estimate the distance from our starting point (km 41.5) to the farthest end of the tidal area (km 44), which is 2.5 km.

4. How much time do we need to hike this distance? Next, we calculate the amount of time we will need to hike that distance.

GOOD TO KNOW! The speed at which one hikes varies depending on terrain, ability, and other factors. You'll be slower when you hike uphill, if the terrain is more technical, if you carry a large load, if you're less in shape, and if you're tired. In general, the average hiker takes about half an hour to hike 1 km (0.62 mile) of a moderate hike. On more technical and challenging route sections, and carrying a pack, the average hiker will take about 1-2 hours to cover the same distance.

In this example, we are trekking along the beach, so we will be hiking about 1 km every half hour. So, hiking 2.5 km should take us about 1 hour and 15 min.

5. What time should we leave our starting point to safely pass the tidal obstacle? Finally, we consult our tide table to see when low tide is occurring, and we count backwards to determine what time to leave our starting point. Remember that the tidal obstacle is passable at tides below 7 ft/ 2.1 m.

Event Date	00	01	02	03	04	05	06	07	08	09	10	11	12	13	14	15	16	17	18	19	20	21	22	23
2024-08-14		1.3	1.1	1.1	1.2	1.4	1.6	1.9	2.2	2.3	2.3	2.3	2.2	2	2	2.1	2.3	2.6	2.9	3	3	2.8	2.5
2024-08-15	2.1	1.6	1.2	1	0.9	1	1.2	1.5	1.9	2.2	2.4	2.5	2.4	2.3	2.1	2	2	2.1	2.3	2.6	2.9	3.1	3.1	2.9
2024-08-16	2.5	2.1	1.5	1.1	0.8	0.7	0.8	1.1	1.5	1.9	2.3	2.6	2.7	2.5	2.3	2.1	1.9	1.9	2	2.3	2.6	3	3.2	3.3
2024-08-17	3	2.6	2	1.4	0.9	0.6	0.5	0.6	1	1.5	2.1	2.5	2.8	2.8	2.6	2.3	1.9	1.7	1.7	1.9	2.2	2.7	3.1	3.4
2024-08-18	3.4	3.1	2.6	1.9	1.2	0.7	0.3	0.3	0.6	1.1	1.7	2.3	2.8	3	2.9	2.5	2.1	1.7	1.5	1.5	1.7	2.2	2.8	3.3
2024-08-19	3.6	3.5	3.2	2.5	1.7	1	0.5	0.2	0.3	0.6	1.3	2	2.7	3.1	3.2	2.9	2.4	1.9	1.5	1.2	1.3	1.6	2.2	2.8
2024-08-20	3.4	3.7	3.6	3.1	2.3	1.5	0.8	0.3	0.1	0.4	0.9	1.6	2.4	3	3.4	3.3	2.8	2.2	1.6	1.2	1	1.1	1.6	2.2
2024-08-21	2.9																							

Let's say we are hiking this path on our fourth day on the trail. We look at the tide table and see that, for August 17, the tide will be below 7 ft/ 2.1 meters before 1000 and after 1530 (although the tide does not increase nor decrease in a completely linear fashion, you can interpolate these data for the sake of estimation). Since the tidal spot is at the start of our hike for the day, we should aim to be at the end of the tidal zone before 1000 to give us plenty of time to complete the trek we planned for the day. Since we determined that hiking past the tidal obstacle will take us 1 hour and 15 min, the latest we should leave camp is 0845. Building in some buffer time, I would aim to leave camp at 0815.

CONSIDER... Make sure to give yourself plenty of time to get to the tidal obstacle. In this example, I gave half an hour of buffer time as I prefer to "do my waiting on the other end" – leave the campsite earlier and wait at the tidal spot for the tide to go out, if necessary (not the case for this particular example as the tide is coming in). This way, we have buffer time built in should anything happen along the way – say, someone falls, gets hurt, and we need to stop for a moment to collect ourselves. The buffer time I build in depends on the terrain and the distance. I give more buffer time for complex terrain, if there are features such as cable cars, and for a greater distance between the starting point and tidal zone. Having buffer time also accounts for any errors in our estimation of the distance between our starting point and the tidal obstacle.

Phew! That was a lot to digest. But, if you take things step by step the way I outlined, you should pass that tidal spot with time to spare. If you get held up and miss the morning low tide, you're lucky that the next low tide is early afternoon and you can pass the spot then. Depending on the trek you had planned for your day, this later crossing might mean you have to set up camp sooner along your itinerary and hike a longer day the next day to catch up, or you tack on an extra day at the end of your hike (which is why we advise having a flexible schedule when you take on a thru-hike).

Chapter Seven

Planning Your Trip in 12 Easy Steps

In this chapter, I lay out the 12 steps involved in planning your multi-day hike and I provide a timeframe for completing each step. Here is an overview of the timeline you can refer to as we go along.

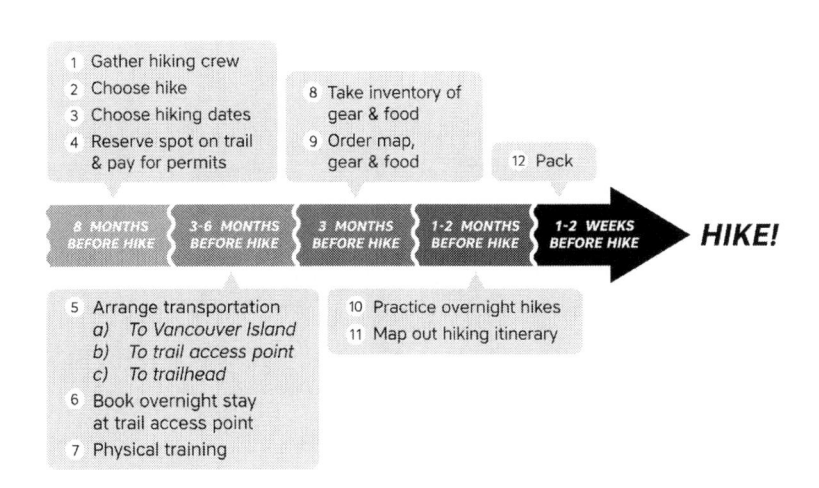

1. Gather hiking crew
2. Choose hike
3. Choose hiking dates
4. Reserve spot on trail & pay for permits
8. Take inventory of gear & food
9. Order map, gear & food
12. Pack

8 MONTHS BEFORE HIKE → **3-6 MONTHS BEFORE HIKE** → **3 MONTHS BEFORE HIKE** → **1-2 MONTHS BEFORE HIKE** → **1-2 WEEKS BEFORE HIKE** → ***HIKE!***

5. Arrange transportation
   a) *To Vancouver Island*
   b) *To trail access point*
   c) *To trailhead*
6. Book overnight stay at trail access point
7. Physical training
10. Practice overnight hikes
11. Map out hiking itinerary

1. GATHER YOUR HIKING CREW (up to 8 months before hike)

You are safer hiking in a group of 4 or more, but it is advised to keep your group size at a maximum of 10. Herding any more people can prove difficult as large groups tend to travel more slowly, and the group dynamic is trickier to keep harmonized. Note that the WCT allows a maximum of 10 hikers per group, and you will need to know their full name and emergency contact information when you reserve your spot on the trail. You'll also need to know your group size when reserving transportation (ferry, water taxi, etc.).

2. CHOOSE YOUR HIKE (up to 8 months before hike)

To help select your hike, it might be useful to ask yourself the following questions:

- Do you want to tackle a world-renowned hike like the WCT or do you want to be more remote and see fewer people?

- How much of a challenge do you want?

- How much distance do you want to cover?

- How many days do you want to be out in the wild?

- How many days can you be away from family or work?

Check out the table in Chapter 10 for a summary of hike details. If you'd rather a shorter hike with fewer tidal obstacles, then the Nootka Trail is your hike. If you want the experience of hiking many types of challenging terrains but don't have a full week, perhaps consider the Tatchu trail.

Theoretically, you can choose and plan your hike at the last minute (except the WCT), but you want to make sure you have ample time to make the required reservations and prepare for the hike, so I suggest choosing your hike by the winter or spring of the same year. Out of excitement for our next adventure, my hiking crew and I typically choose our next hike within a month of finishing the year's trek – a year in advance! This timing gives us plenty of time to choose our dates, book time off work, and make all the arrangements necessary. Plus, starting to plan this early on gives us a big adventure to look forward to all year round!

3. CHOOSE YOUR HIKING DATES (up to 8 months before hike)

The trails mentioned in this guidebook are open from May 1 to September 30.

PRO TIP: When choosing your hike dates, consider the month for factors such as daylight, daytime and nighttime temperatures, precipitation and other weather conditions, tide heights, fire ban, etc.

Hiking in June means you have the most daylight hours, but it might mean you get more rain. However, campfires are usually still allowed in June. Hiking in August, on the other hand, might mean the weather and trail are dryer, but it might also mean there's a fire ban in place. We hiked the WCT late September and it rained 4 of the 7 days we were on the trail, which is not ideal. But, we ran into fewer people as the trail was winding down for the season and therefore less busy.

Also, the length of your hike will help determine the number of days you should take to complete it, depending on the distance you want to hike each day. We typically aim to hike a max of 10-12 km (6-7.5 miles) per day, depending on where the campsites are located and the type of terrain we cover any given day. This distance translates to about 5-12 hours per day, depending on the type of terrain covered.

4. RESERVE YOUR SPOT ON THE TRAIL & PAY FOR PERMITS (up to 8 months before hike)

Nootka Trail. The Nootka Trail requires you to pay for a group landing fee and a hiking permit, payable ahead of time online (https://explorenootka.com/pf/hiking/) or in person, in cash, on the trail.

North Coast & Cape Scott Trail. The North Coast & Cape Scott Trail also requires a camping permit, payable ahead of time online (https://camping.bcparks.ca/; select Backcountry, Backcountry Registration, and input your dates and name of park: Cape Scott). The fees can also be paid in person at the trailhead, or at the Quarterdeck Marina (where you catch a water taxi or bus shuttle to one of the trailheads).

Tatchu Trail. The Tatchu Trail does not require a camping permit nor does it have camping fees.

West Coast Trail. The WCT is the only hike mentioned in this guidebook that requires you to reserve so far in advance. You can create an account and reserve here: https://reservation.pc.gc.ca/. Reservations typically open in the winter and are on a first-come, first-served basis. Spots fill up incredibly quickly so it's imperative to create an account ahead of time and log onto the system before registration opens. Make sure you're flexible with your travel dates as you might not get the dates you originally planned. For this hike, you pay all your fees at the time of registration.

5. ARRANGE TRANSPORTATION (3-6 months before hike)

Travel can be booked as soon as you know your hiking dates. There should be no problem reserving for the dates you want as long as you reserve far enough in advance.

Below is a map of Vancouver Island with markers showing the trailheads, trails, some campsites, and options for transportation.

BACKPACKING VANCOUVER ISLAND 101

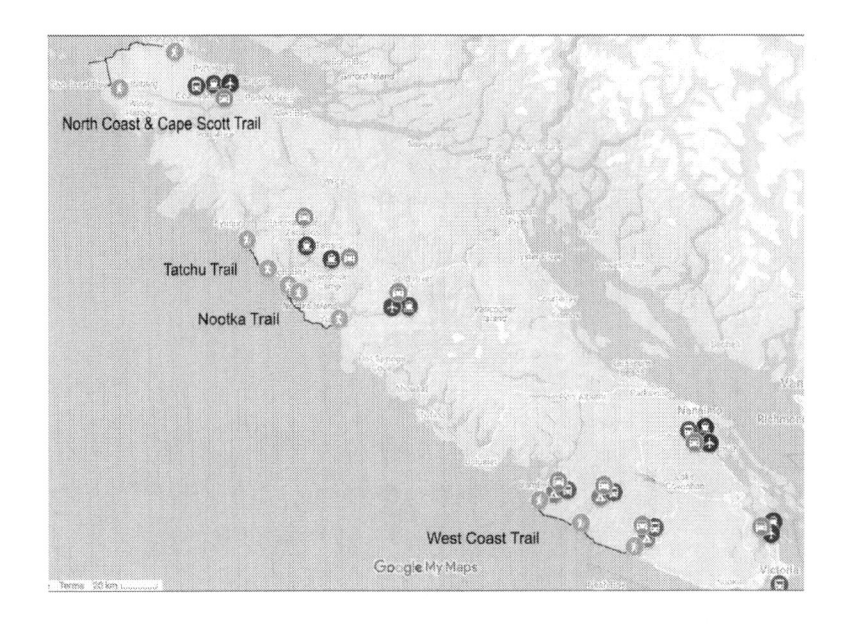

[Map showing Vancouver Island with labeled trails: North Coast & Cape Scott Trail, Tatchu Trail, Nootka Trail, and West Coast Trail]

a) Transportation to Vancouver Island. If you're flying to Vancouver Island, fly into the closest city to your trail access point (town/ marina closest to the trailhead). If you're hiking the Nootka or Tatchu Trails, fly into Nanaimo. For the North Coast & Cape Scott Trail, fly into Port Hardy. If you're hiking the West Coast Trail, fly into either Nanaimo or Victoria.

You can also take a ferry from Vancouver to Vancouver Island, either to Victoria or Nanaimo. Note that, for vehicle passengers, the ferry sells out during the summer months so if you will be driving on, be sure to reserve early.

b) Transportation to the trail access point. Once you get to Vancouver Island, you will need transportation to get to the trail access point. For the Nootka and Tatchu Trails, trail access points are in Tahsis, Zeballos, and Gold River. The trail access point for the North Coast & Cape Scott Trail is Port Hardy. If you're hiking the WCT, the trail access points are either Port Renfrew, Nitinat, or Bamfield, depending on where you start the hike.

One option is to drive a car from the airport/ ferry terminal to the trail access point. If you're hiking the WCT, another option is to take a shuttle bus from the Nanaimo ferry terminal or from the Victoria Capital City bus station (for this option, keep in mind that you will also have to find transportation from the Nanaimo airport to the ferry terminal or from the Victoria airport/ ferry to the bus station). The West Coast Trail shuttle bus also travels between the three trailheads (in the event that you drive to one end, finish at the other, and need to get back to your car), and can be reserved at https://trailbus.com/.

c) Transportation to trailhead. The Nootka and Tatchu trails are water taxi or float plane access. You can reserve a water taxi trip with Zeballos Expeditions at https://www.zeballosexpeditions.com/transportation.html

or with Shorebird Expeditions at https://shorebirdexpeditions.com/expeditions/hike-nootka-sound/.

The crew on a Shorebird water taxi, feeling pumped about having just completed the Nootka Trail. From left to right: Wade, Dylan, Graig, Jré, Abra, Kyle, me, and Drew.

You can also book a float plane with Air Nootka at https://www.airnootka.com/hiking. Flying to the trailhead has its advantages, such as shorter travel time and breathtaking views of your trek, but it is more expensive and the plane will be grounded during bad weather, so your dates should be flexible if you choose this mode of transportation.

For the North Coast & Cape Scott Trail, you'll need to book a water taxi and shuttle with Cape Scott Water Taxi & North Coast Trail Shuttle: https://www.capescottwatertaxi.ca/.

The WCT has three trailheads, two of which require a water taxi to access (Nitinat and Port Renfrew; reservations for this water taxi are made when you reserve your spot on the trail). The third trailhead (Bamfield) is accessible from the campground parking lot.

6. ARRANGE OVERNIGHT STAY AT TRAIL ACCESS POINT (3-6 months before hike)

No matter where you're traveling from, it'll take you the better part of a day just to get to the trail access point. You'll want to arrange an overnight stay here so you can catch transportation (water taxi or float plane) to the trailhead the next day (typically early in the morning to take advantage of calmer water). Accommodations can be booked as soon as you know your hike start date.

For the Nootka and Tatchu trails, you can stay the night in Tahsis, Zeballos or Gold River; Shorebird Expeditions, Zeballos Expeditions, and Air Nootka depart from these locations. Parking is available for a fee. When my crew and I hiked the Nootka and Tatchu trails, we stayed the night in Tahsis (once at the Tahsis Westview Marina, https://www.westviewmarina.com/) and we took the water taxi from the marina the next morning.

For the North Coast & Cape Scott Trail, a stay in Port Hardy will do the trick. You'll be catching the water taxi or shuttle bus from the Quarterdeck Inn & Marina; they also offer parking for a fee.

For the WCT, each trailhead has a campground: the Pachena Bay Campground in Bamfield, the Nitinat Lake Recreation Site in Nitinat, and the Pacheedaht Campground in Port Renfrew. Depending on your timing and entry point, you can start the hike when you arrive or spend the night should you wish to rest from your travels and start your journey fresh the next morning. The Nitinat and Pacheedaht trailheads require a boat ride to the hike, so you may have to wait until the next day anyway. Alternatively, if you have your own car, you can stay somewhere nearby and drive to the trailhead the next morning, where there is paid parking.

7. PHYSICAL TRAINING (3-6 months before hike, depending on current level of fitness and training regime)

As I mentioned previously, I trained for my first thru-hike for a few months. Before this intentional training, I played tennis at least twice per week so my cardio was already on point. But, I needed to train my body to haul a heavy pack up and down ladders and hills, so I went on one hike per week for three months in addition to playing tennis. As I got stronger, I loaded my backpack with weight and went on more challenging hikes. For me, this regime was sufficient to prepare me for the WCT.

Consider your current level of fitness and the kind of training strategy and schedule that is realistic for you. Maybe you go to the gym three times per week for a few months. Whatever your regime, make sure you're working your main muscles as well as the accessory muscles used in hiking.

8. TAKE INVENTORY OF YOUR HIKING GEAR AND FOOD (3 months before hike)

Go through your checklists in Chapter 10 and take note of what you have and what you need to get. If you're opting to make your own meals and dehydrate, you should start that process now.

GOOD TO KNOW! Note that if you're partnering up for the trail, you only need one tent, one stove, one tarp, etc. between the two of you. So it might be useful to go through your inventory with your partner and note what you still need between the two of you.

9. ORDER MAP, GEAR AND FOOD (3 months before hike)

You can get a map of the hikes I cover in this guidebook here: https://www.wildisle.ca/coastalmaps/index.html?ls=1&mt=11

and

https://store.avenza.com/products/pacific-rim-national-park-west-coast-trail-part-1-parks-canada-map.

For gear and food, you can order most of what you need online, but if you need a backpack, I suggest you go into a retailer and speak with their specialists to make sure they size it correctly with you. A properly fitting backpack is key for comfort and, ultimately, for your enjoyment on the trail. You'll want to gather your backpacking gear early enough so that you can go on practice overnight hikes and test out your gear before your thru-hike.

10. PRACTICE OVERNIGHT HIKES (1-2 months before hike)

Once you gather your gear, it's time to go on a couple practice overnight hikes! The main goals of this exercise are to test your gear, go through the process of hiking in, setting up camp etc, and hiking out, and to test your physical ability after having trained for a few months or more. The more similar the overnight hike is to the multi-day trek you're planning, the better prepared you will be. An app like AllTrails is useful when researching hikes (https://www.alltrails.com/). You can search by geographical area, length, and difficulty of hike, along with other criteria.

11. MAP YOUR HIKING ITINERARY (1-2 months before hike)

Before making a plan, I read blog posts and other material about the hike, including the writings on the map itself. I gather information on the difficulty of the hike, the topography, the campsites, tricky areas, water sources, tides, and points of interest. With this information, I can choose our direction of travel, I know the number of days needed to hike the trail, I know our tidal data, and I know which campsites are preferred. Once you collect this information, you can map your hiking itinerary.

Which direction to hike? Typically, one end of the trail is more difficult than the other, so be strategic on how to approach your hiking journey.

GOOD TO KNOW! Your pack will get a little lighter each day you hike as you're consuming food; by the end of your week-long hike, your pack will weigh about 10-15 pounds less.

CONSIDER… Consider whether you want to complete the hard section at the start of your hike (which means you're well rested and not sore), or if you'd rather hike the harder part with less weight on your back (at the end of the hike). Also consider that you will be more tired at the end of your hike and that accidents are more likely to occur as a result of being tired. So, if you'd prefer to hit the tough sections while you're fresh and not so tired or sore, start with the tougher section. My hiking crew and I prefer to start with the hard section.

How much hiking to do per day? Divide the distance of the trail by the number of days you have to get an average number of miles/ kilometres you need to hike per day. For the week-long hikes mentioned here, you'll be hiking 5-10 km (3-6 miles) per day, which is roughly 5-12 hours per day. If you want a more leisurely hike, you can certainly hike a shorter distance every day, but you'll need to give yourself more days to finish the hike. Remember to give yourself more time to hike more difficult terrain (ie., forest sections, hills) and to cross any tidal obstacles.

Where are the tidal obstacles? Note where the tidal obstacles are; your map will indicate these sections. Refer to your tide table (see Chapter 6 for instructions on how to find, read, and use a tide table), and note the time(s) of the day during which a safe passage is feasible. Note that the times will differ a little each day. With the tide information, you can strategically plan when to hike through the obstacle and also where to set up camp relative to the obstacle.

Where do we camp? Your map will show the trail's campsites and whether they have an outhouse and a food/ bear cache. Camp at sites that have reliable access to fresh water.

PRO TIP: Look at blog posts to gather information about camp sites. Doing some research here can give you a feel for ideal spots to set up camp, whether on the beach or in the forest. You'll also read whether the water source at any given site is reliable or if it has dried out at certain times of the year.

GOOD TO KNOW! If camping on the beach, remember to set up your tent *above* the high tide line or you might wake up in the middle of the night laying in a water bed. You can spot the high tide line in the sand as a line of kelp, seaweed, and other ocean debris left over from the last high tide. When in doubt, set up your tent further up the beach, farther away from the water.

Points of interest. As you research the trail you'd like to take on, you might come across certain points that pique your interest. Mark these points on your map so you're sure to look out for them along your trek.

I organize my itinerary by day. For each day, I mark the start and end points and the hiking distance and time. I also make notes on the water sources, the tidal obstacles, or other trail features (such as cable cars).

Once I have my itinerary ironed out, I transfer the information to my waterproof map. Here is a section of my map for the North Coast & Cape Scott Trail:

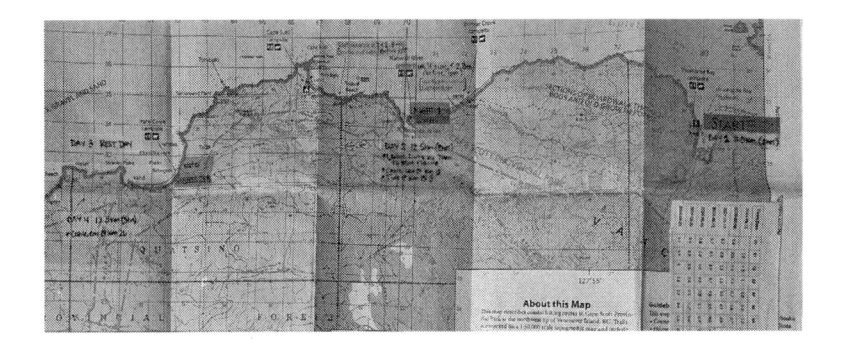

As I mentioned, I tape over the entire tide table (lower right) with packing tape so it, too, is waterproof. I then use sticky tabs to indicate each hiking day's itinerary: the distance we are covering, the campsites we will stay at, tidal obstacles, points of interest, etc. When necessary, I also indicate the time we need to leave camp in the morning in order to beat a tidal obstacle. I then tape over the sticky tabs with packing tape so they stay in place and are also waterproof.

Of course, the itinerary is subject to change when on the trail, but it's nice to have a general plan in place, and having the tide table on the map means you can adjust your itinerary on-the-go, if required.

12. PACK YOUR BACKPACK (1-2 weeks before hike)

I like to give myself a couple of weeks to pack so that if I forgot to buy anything, I still have plenty of time to do so. In the next chapter, I provide a long list of items you want to consider bringing along. Some items are essential while others are luxury or personal preference (again, going on practice overnight hikes will help you decide what is necessary to you). I also provide guidance on how to pack your backpack to ensure you are set up for comfort and convenience.

When I pack for my hike, I like to divide my checklist list into sections, and I usually collect items within a section and pack them together. For example, I keep all of my clothes in one bag, my food and food hanging kit in another bag, etc. Note that these items in particular go in dry compression bags.

GOOD TO KNOW! The thought behind what to put in a dry bag is this: if I fall into the river and my pack gets soaked, what can I *not* afford to be wet? Answer: my sleeping bag, my clothes, and my food. So, I have three separate dry compression bags. (A plastic garbage bag does the trick but is more prone to tears).

I start by preparing my food bag, my emergency/ first aid kit, my clothes, then I gather the camping items I want to bring. I lay everything out in front of me and I check items off my checklist as I pack them. It's important to pack your backpack properly so that you avoid injury and so you can access certain items quickly (ie., without taking off your pack or without needing to unpack to get at these items). More on how to pack your backpack in Chapter 9.

Chapter Eight

What to Pack

Thinking about what to bring on your first multi-day backpacking trip can be overwhelming. You need to think about the different scenarios you will find yourself in and pack accordingly (hiking, at camp, cooking, sleeping, etc). In this section, I provide a list and description of many possible items one could bring – some are necessary and others are nice to have. You can find a simple checklist of these items in Chapter 10. Remember, the more items you bring, the more luxurious your camping experience, but the heavier your pack will be. As I mentioned previously, it is highly recommended to complete at least one overnight hike before attempting a multi-day hike. The more overnight hikes you do, the more you will know what *you* deem necessary and what you can leave behind to save on weight and space.

HIKING

Hiking clothes. First, ditch all of your cotton clothes in favour of merino wool, nylon, or polyester. When wet, cotton stays cold and it takes a while to dry, whereas wool and other synthetics will wick moisture away and keep you warm even if wet. Underwear, sports bra, pants/ shorts/ skort, socks – none of these should be made with cotton. Remember to bring multiple layers if you're expecting different temperatures and weather conditions. For more information, visit https://www.rei.com/learn/expert-advice/how-to-choose-hiking-clothes.html.

Hiking shoes. I love my hiking boots – they're sturdy, have great tread (grip underfoot), they've got ankle support, and they dry quickly. Others opt for trail runners, even though they might not be as durable, or hiking sandals. Either way, your footwear should provide support, protection from rocks and roots, and traction on wet and dry surfaces. Whatever you do, save yourself the pain and wear-in your shoes *before* your backpacking trip.

* GAME CHANGER * I tape up my feet on day 1 of the hike, *before* blisters form.

Backpack & rain cover. Being comfortable while carrying 30-45 pounds on your back for several days is mandatory. A sore back can quickly change morale and affect the enjoyment of your trip. For a multi-day hike (3+ nights), your backpack should be 60-80 litres in capacity. When choosing a backpack, consider features like fit, comfort, capacity, storage compartments, pack access, pockets, and attachment points. I will cover what goes in the backpack and how to pack it in later sections. Visit https://www.rei.com/learn/expert-advice/backpack.html for more information.

Backpacks typically come with a rain cover that fits snugly around the outside of your pack and keeps it dry (ish) in rainy conditions.

PRO TIP: I bought a larger rain cover to ensure anything clipped to the outside of my pack also fits under the cover. No regrets. (In general, though, it is better *not* to have anything dangling off your pack. The dangling item can throw off your balance or get caught on something).

Hiking poles. I consider hiking poles to be a complete * GAME CHANGER * and I would not go on a moderate or challenging hike without them. They are helpful for both uphill and downhill sections; they help with balance and weight distribution as you can put your weight into them when high stepping, they catch you if you stumble, they help protect the knees, and you can use them to clear bushes or branches out of your path. You can also use them to test the sturdiness of a log or root or whatever platform you want to step onto next, or to test the depth of a water or mud puddle. When hiking alone or in small groups, you can bang your poles together to make noise to alert wildlife of your presence. Hiking poles can also serve as protection against an animal, should you need it. Finally, your poles can be used to prop up a tarp at camp.

Bear spray. The canister should be accessible, held in a holster along your waist or chest strap. (My hiking comrade, Wade, once left his bear spray *inside* his backpack... some other item depressed the canister's trigger and it sprayed the inside of his pack. It's a good thing his clothes and food were inside a dry bag!)

Accessories for protection. Sunglasses, a hat, and sunscreen protect you from the sun. Gloves keep your hands warm and protect against scrapes and bugs. Gaiters protect your shins and ankles against bumps, scrapes, and bugs, and prevent debris from entering your shoes. Refrain from wearing any fashion accessories that dangle as they could get caught on something and hurt you or break off.

Phone/ camera protection accessory. During your trek, you might want your cell phone or camera to be accessible so you can take pictures along the way. I keep my phone in a cell phone-sized dry bag, tied to an adjustable lanyard that can be hung across my chest or waist. I wear mine like a necklace/ chain, and it rests on top of my clothes so it's easily accessible. The pouch is clear so the phone screen is visible, and the touchscreen still works through the plastic. All the while, your phone is protected from bumps, scratches, water, and other elements. Note that the phone/ camera might swing across your body as you hike (which gets in the way), so I just tuck mine under my hip belt, against my abdomen and it stays put.

Waterproof map & tide table. Make sure your map is waterproof or it will disintegrate if it rains. I use packing tape to tape the tide table to my map; I cover the paper entirely so it is also protected from the rain.

Fanny pack. This is where I store my map, snacks, water purification tablets, medication, and anything else I might need easy access to while hiking.

WATER & FILTRATION/ PURIFICATION

As I mentioned previously, you'll need a filtration/ purification system to clean your drinking water. I use a combination of filters and tablets, depending on whether I am at camp or on the go. Filtration and purification systems worth considering can be read about and compared here: https://www.rei.com/learn/expert-advice/water-treatment-backcountry.html.

SHELTER/ SLEEPING

Tent. My hiking partner and I share a 3-person tent and it's large enough for 2 people plus our backpacks. A 2-person tent would be a bit too tight, but some prefer to be snug and save on the weight that a larger tent comes with.

Tent footprint. A footprint is useful to protect your tent from moisture and debris on the ground.

Tarp. I've camped in the rain without a tarp and, guess what: the inside of your waterproof tent does get moist. So, I invested in a tarp for extra shelter from the elements. If you invest in a tarp, make sure it is lightweight and large enough to cover what you need covered. I went with a 10' x 10' tarp and it adequately covers my 3-person tent.

CONSIDER... The more lightweight your tarp (or tent/ other gear) is, the more expensive it will be, but sometimes it's worth the extra cost to keep the weight of your backpack down.

Sleeping pad/ ground mat. A sleeping pad is essential for comfort but also protects your body from the cold, wet, uneven ground. There are inflatable mats, self-inflating mats, foams, and mats that come with foot pumps. Do your research and make sure the mat you get is large enough for your body. Your mat can also be used as a chair around camp.

Sleeping bag. Your sleeping bag should keep you warm overnight, so make sure to get one with the correct temperature rating, along with the correct sizing for your body, packability, and desired weight. I store my sleeping bag in a dry compression bag.

Pillow. I've tried camping with a small, packable pillow and I've gone without. To save on weight and space, I typically forgo the pillow and just fluff up my clothes bag and use it as a pillow.

Eye mask & ear plugs. If you're sensitive to the morning light, bring an eye mask. If you're easily awakened by your hiking partner's snoring, bring ear plugs. Both are lightweight, can easily fit anywhere, and have a tremendously positive impact on sleep quality.

CLOTHES

Consider packing your clothes in a dry compression bag (a plain garbage bag works fine, too).

Fleece/ thermal top & pants. For cooler temperatures.

Socks. Wool only; 2 pairs for hiking, 1 thick pair for camp/ nighttime, 1 extra pair.

Down Jacket. For cooler temperatures. Can be used as a pillow if not worn overnight.

Rain jacket & rain pants. I usually check the weather forecast before my hike to know whether to pack these items. They're useful when it rains, but they add significant weight to your pack so I leave them behind if the forecast isn't predicting showers.

Toque/ beanie & gloves. For cooler temperatures. Can be used as a pillow if not worn overnight.

Second top & bottoms. I carry an extra top and bottoms because they're nice to have when you're not hiking and the temperature is still warm.

FOOTWEAR

Shoes/ sandals for camp. The lighter the better; avoid thongs or sandals that separate your toes if you will wear socks with sandals.

Water shoes. For river/ creek crossings.

KITCHEN

Stove, fuel, & lighter. How much fuel do you need? Well, for 7 days, my hiking partner and I have enough of two 230-g isobutane fuel cartridges (or one 450 g cartridge). We use fuel to cook breakfasts, dinners, and warm drinks.

Pot, bowl, cup. I have a larger pot (almost 2 L/ about 65 ounces) and it's large enough to cook a meal for two people, or boil enough water to rehydrate two meals and make a couple cups of tea.

Utensils. I use a metal spoon with a long handle. I've tried various sporks and they've all disappointed: either the spoon part doesn't hold the liquid, or the fork part doesn't pick up food, or the mechanism to fold the spork is too sensitive so it folds while I'm stirring food, or my fingers get burned when I use the spork to eat out of a rehydratable meal bag because the handle is too short for the spork to reach the bottom of the bag without me sticking my fingers in the bag... and that's why I opted for a metal spoon with a long handle.

Biodegradable soap. You don't need to use that much, a few drops will do for a few dishes.

Aeropress & filters. For coffee drinkers.

FOOD

As I mentioned earlier, your food should be stored in a dry bag. How much food do you need? Well, that depends on the number of calories you need to consume, which depends on your size, weight, and the type of hiking you are planning on any given day. In general, you need about 1½ to 2½ pounds of food (or 2,500 to 4,500 calories) per day. I pack more food for days where the hiking is more intense, and for rest days (you'll be surprisingly hungry on rest days; thanks for the tip, Jré!).

Breakfast. From on-the-go protein shakes and bars to cooking omelettes or oatmeal, your breakfast of choice might be based on preference and/or the type of morning you plan on having. When I have time at camp in the morning, I try to eat a hearty oatmeal breakfast before hiking. But, if I need to wake up very early and need to rush out of camp to beat a tidal obstacle, I will opt for a bar on the go. So, I make sure to pack accordingly.

Lunch. I only pack a hot lunch for rest days. On hiking days, I make due with snacks to avoid the hassle of unpacking my kitchen, cooking, cleaning, and repacking on our short lunch breaks.

Dinner. I am a huge fan of dehydrated meal packs. My hiking comrade Abra makes all of her meals and dehydrates them herself, which ends up saving money. I followed suit one year and I found the process to be too time consuming, so I now opt to spend the $20-25 per dinner to save on time and effort (I also save on having to do dishes as I only need my cooking pot for boiling water instead of needing to heat my meal in it).

GOOD TO KNOW! If you opt for pre-made, dehydrated meal packs, make sure you're getting around 30 g of protein per meal. Read the label carefully; many packs will advertise as "2 servings" when in fact it's one dinner for one hungry hiker.

Treats. Optional, but they don't take up much room and a couple of single-serve chocolates per night really elevates your camping experience.

Drinks. Other than water, which you collect along your journey, I like to bring different powdered drink options to keep things interesting. I bring coffee, tea, electrolytes, and hot chocolate and I savour every warm sip of tea or hot cocoa while I sit around the fire on a cool night.

I like to package each day's meals together. So, for a 7-day hike, I have 7 large ziplock bags, each containing the day's rations.

Compared to having a dry bag full of random food items, this method is much more organized and it saves time and effort at mealtime. Also, having your food already portioned out for you avoids dipping into your future stash when you're hungry. In the morning, I take out the day's ziplock bag, I pull out the snacks I have for the day, and I store them in my fanny pack or my backpack's hip belt pockets so they're easily accessible while hiking.

PRO TIP: You'll be hungrier than you think on days where you're not hiking, so pack extra food for days off.

CONSIDER... Consider packing one extra day's worth of meals. That way, you are covered if you need to extend your trip, if your fellow hiker didn't pack enough food, or if your water taxi pickup on the last day is late/ not coming because of bad weather conditions. (Remember earlier when I mentioned that we aimed to complete the WCT in 6 days but because of bad weather we needed 7 days? Well, the truth is, we hadn't packed extra food, which was a rookie mistake. Luckily, we made friends with a solo German hiker who ended up joining our crew and she had plenty of food to share. Phew! Thanks, Kathrina! We now always pack an extra day's worth of food – and we needed that extra ration one year when my hike mate Wade spilled his dinner all over the sand, which happened shortly after he discovered that his bag was soaked with bear spray. What a day! We give Wade much credit for keeping his composure and for remaining positive despite these challenges.)

Visit https://www.rei.com/learn/expert-advice/planning-menu.html for more information on meal planning and meal ideas.

TOILETRIES

Toothbrush, toothpaste, & floss. Even though you're out in the wild, you should still care for your oral hygiene. Make sure to get a travel-sized, biodegradable toothpaste.

Deodorant/ antiperspirant. Optional, but often discouraged because the smell attracts animals. If you do wear some, don't apply right before bed when the smell will be the strongest.

Hair brush & elastics (optional).

Lotion, sunscreen & insect repellant. Think small containers to save on weight and space.

Feminine hygiene products. Remember to pack them out with you after use.

Biodegradable toilet paper. For a week-long hike, I typically bring about 1.5 rolls, although 1 roll would probably suffice. I like the motto "it's better to have it and not need it, than need it and not have it," and toilet paper is light enough that adding half a roll doesn't make a huge impact on pack weight.

Biodegradable wipes. Like I mentioned previously, I like to give myself a sponge bath after a day's hike. I pack the wipes out with me.

Sanitizer. Remember - there is no running water so use sanitizer after nature calls.

Medications. Any medication you currently take plus antihistamines, painkillers, and anti-inflammatory medication, if needed.

GEAR

GPS (global positioning system) receiver. This device shows the map of your hike, where you are along your trek, and you can use it to send messages and updates to loved ones. It comes in handy if you're lost or if you're tracking your hike. For more information on GPS receivers, visit: https://www.rei.com/learn/expert-advice/gps-receiver.html#:~:text=Once%20revolutionary%2C%20GPS%20technology%20is,where%20you%20want%20to%20go.

CAUTION! Never rely solely on this (or any) electronic device as it can fail. Make sure to also have a waterproof map and compass, and know how to read both.

Rope/ paracord. You'll need about 40 feet of rope to hang your bear bag. Having some extra paracord handy (15 ft) can come through in a pinch as you can set up a clothesline to dry your wet clothes, hang a tarp, replace a broken shoelace, etc.

Carabiners. You need a strong, locking carabiner for your bear bag setup, but otherwise, you do not need climbing grade carabiners to hang items inside your tent, for instance.

Tarp. Handy as a sun blocker or a shelter from the rain, make sure your tarp comes with pegs and straps/ rope (or cut pieces of your paracord).

Headlamp. An absolutely necessary piece of gear. Get a headlamp with a few brightness settings and a red light; bugs are not attracted to red light and it's easier on everyone's eyes.

Battery pack (optional). I carry one to recharge my headlamp and my phone.

Knife. A knife is an essential survival tool as it can be used to build a shelter, make fire, prepare food, craft tools, cut rope, and it can be used for first aid and self-defense.

MISCELLANEOUS

Trowel. If the trail you're hiking does not have outhouses, you will need to bring a trowel (or at least one person in your group needs to). See Chapter 4 for details on digging a "cathole" and going to the bathroom in the woods.

Towel (optional). Can also be used as a pillow or a blanket.

PRO TIP: If you find that your sleeping bag slides around on your sleeping mat, lay a towel between your mat and sleeping bag and you will no longer slide.

Chair (optional). I bring a light camping chair but I've also used a gardener's foam knee pad to sit on in lieu of a chair. Although the knee pad is lighter, the chair is much more comfortable.

Small backpack for day hikes. Handy if you have a rest day built into your itinerary.

GOOD TO KNOW! The brain – top compartment – of some backpacks detaches and forms a small pack.

Musical instrument/ speaker. If you want to listen to music around camp, bring a speaker or an instrument. One year, we had a didgeridoo and a ukulele, which really complemented our camp experience (thanks to Kioshi and Dylan for their musical stylings; these two are featured on this book's cover).

Fairy lights. I like to set up fairy lights in my tent for ambiance and so I can find it after dark (your headlamp's light only shines so far).

Hand/ feet warmers. These come in handy on a cold, rainy night. Stick a few in your sleeping bag for extra warmth.

Cash. The West Coast Trail has a shack at its midway point – the Crab Shack – where you can buy food and other supplies and where you can rent a cabin. Their prices are steep and they only accept cash, so bring a couple hundred dollars just in case you do want to spend the night and stock up on supplies.

When we hiked the WCT, we arrived at the Crab Shack in the middle of the heaviest rainstorms I have ever witnessed (akin to Arizona's monsoon, which I have also witnessed). We and our packs were completely soaked so we stayed the night in one of their cabins. We set up several clotheslines (with our paracord!) and used their heaters to dry everything we had, from our clothes to our gear and tents. We were happy to pay the extra dollars for this comfort. (At this point in our journey, my hiking crew had split in two. The other half of our crew had already passed the Crab Shack, but they too were behind on the itinerary and were nowhere near the next campsite. Nightfall was upon them and they needed to set up an emergency shelter — fast [see Chapter 5]. Luckily, they ran into a cave along their path that was large enough for their tents to fit. They were able to have a fire and stay dry for the night. Comparing our different experiences once reunited after the trail made for some great story telling.)

A cave along the WCT that served as an emergency shelter for my crew mates

Extra ziplock/ plastic bags. Useful for containing trash and feminine hygiene products. If you don't want to see the contents of the bag, tape the outside of the bag using duct tape, which also reinforces the bag to prevent tears.

EMERGENCY/ FIRST AID KIT

When packing for a multi-day hike, you should aim to be self-reliant in case of an emergency. When I prepare, I pack with this thought in mind: "If I fall off a cliff or get separated from my crew, do I have what's necessary to survive until I am found?" On these trails, rescue could be a few days away, so let's make sure you are prepared for the worst-case scenario.

Whistle. A must. If you get lost, your cries for help will only be heard so far and you can only yell for so long before your voice gets hoarse.

Emergency blanket. Also a must. Lightweight, compact, and life-saving, the reflective material of an emergency blanket prevents body heat loss and prevents hypothermia.

Knife. A knife is an essential survival tool as it can be used to build a shelter, make fire, prepare food, craft tools, cut rope, and it can be used for first aid and self-defense.

Compass. Small and lightweight, a compass is useful if you've gotten lost. Visit https://www.rei.com/learn/expert-advice/navigation-basics.html for a demonstration on how to use a compass.

Mirror. In the event that you are lost, use a mirror to send a light signal to rescuers.

Fire starter and lighter. I like to keep a couple of fire starter sticks in my emergency pack just in case the wood around me is too wet, or in the event that I am alone, hurt, and cannot move to gather wood. I prefer a barbeque lighter to a regular lighter so that I don't burn myself while lighting different points in my fire.

Tealight candles. In the event that you cannot build a fire and you need extra heat, light a few tealight candles and huddle around the flames to keep warm. Just make sure they are scent-free to prevent attracting animals. I keep four tealight candles in my emergency kit.

Water purification tablets. Small and weightless, backup tablets are useful to keep in your emergency kit.

Bandages & blister care. I tape up my feet and toes before blisters form, but if they do form, I'm happy to have the ointment and bandages to protect my skin. See Chapter 5 for how to deal with blisters.

Tweezers. For splinter and tick removal. Some have a small magnifying glass attached to them.

Tape (climber's tape, electrical tape). Climber's tape goes on skin to protect against blisters and other wounds. I also carry a small amount of electrical tape to repair gear.

Gear repair kit. Some gear comes with its own gear repair kit. If not, think about procuring one, as a night sleeping on a deflated ground mat is no fun (isn't that right, Kyle?).

Zip ties. I usually pack a dozen or so. They're useful in many situations (shelter, first aid, gear repair), they take up little space, and they barely weigh anything.

Extra batteries. Pack enough batteries to replenish all devices that need batteries should they all fail at once.

Great! You've assembled everything you need — and hopefully a few luxury items as well. Did you weigh things as you went? Now let's see if it all fits inside your backpack.

Chapter Nine

How to Pack

When we pack, we pack for comfort and convenience. We want to distribute the weight correctly to maintain our centre of gravity, thus decreasing the likelihood of injury and ensuring comfort. We also want particular items to be easily accessible during the hike so that we don't need to take off our pack and unpack to get at them.

Backpacks have different zones, each corresponding to the weight and items occupying that space:

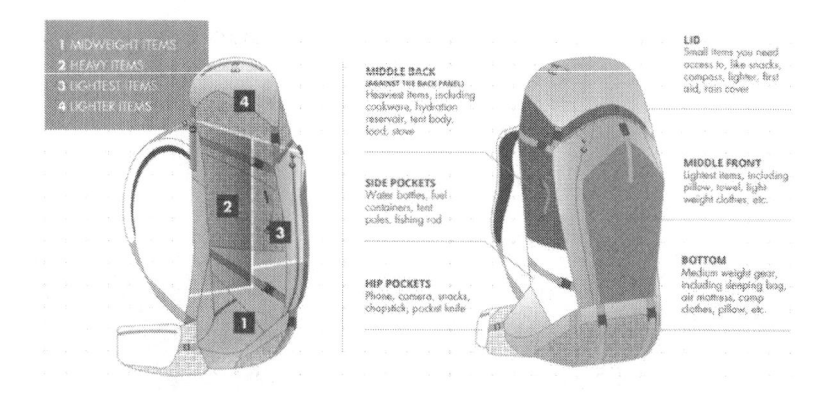

1. MIDWEIGHT ITEMS
2. HEAVY ITEMS
3. LIGHTEST ITEMS
4. LIGHTER ITEMS

MIDDLE BACK (AGAINST THE BACK PANEL)
Heaviest items, including cookware, hydration reservoir, tent body, food, stove

SIDE POCKETS
Water bottles, fuel containers, tent poles, fishing rod

HIP POCKETS
Phone, camera, snacks, chopstick, pocket knife

LID
Small items you need access to, like snacks, compass, lighter, first aid, rain cover

MIDDLE FRONT
Lightest items, including pillow, towel, light weight clothes, etc.

BOTTOM
Medium weight gear, including sleeping bag, air mattress, camp clothes, pillow, etc.

1. Bottom: Midweight items (sleeping bag, ground mat, clothes, pillow);

2. Middle back: Heaviest items (hydration bladder, food, tent, cookware);

3. Middle front: Lightest items (towel, trowel, toilet paper, rain gear, sunscreen, bug spray, water shoes for creek crossings);

4. Top/ lid/ "brain": Lighter items (emergency/ first aid kit, water filter, rain cover, snacks);

5. Open side pockets (water bottle, fuel);

6. Hip pockets (phone, camera, GPS receiver, snacks, knife, headlamp, chapstick);

7. Outside bottom (lengthwise against pack bottom; strapped to backpack using outer compression straps): ground mat, camping chair.

Before packing, lay everything out in front of you. This way, you can see everything and you can run through your checklist one more time. Loosen the compression straps around your backpack and start packing. Start with zone 1 and pack your bag up from there, leaving the open side pockets and hip pockets to the end. Check items off your checklist as you put them in your pack (see next chapter for packing checklist). Finally, once everything is in your pack, tighten the compression straps to hold everything in place.

Now for the moment of truth: try your pack on and see how much it weighs! In general, you want your pack to weigh no more than 20% of your body weight. You might have to leave some luxury items out if your pack is too heavy. If it feels lop-sided or top heavy, you might have to unpack and try again using a different configuration. Just remember that heavy items should go against your back, near your shoulders, to maintain your centre of gravity.

I'm petite so my pack typically weighs around 40% of my body weight. It's not ideal, but doable with proper training and encouragement. The alternative is asking your fellow hike mates to help carry some items, but that's not ideal in the event you get separated. On my first thru-hike, my hike mates were kind enough to each take a day's worth of food, which helped alleviate my load. However, our crew ended up splitting up on day 4 of 7 and I was left without my food (and without my coffee!). Since you're packing to be self-reliant, and you need everything you pack, I wouldn't advise giving items to your hike mates unless you absolutely have to. Learn from my rookie mistake!

PRO TIP: If you have a water bladder that fits into the backside compartment, place it in the backpack first and pack around it (packing the bladder after everything else is much trickier!).

PRO TIP: Pack your food above your fuel canister so if your fuel canister leaks, your food won't be spoiled if it's not in a dry bag.

PRO TIP: If you have a bulky, lightweight item like a foam ground mat or camping chair that doesn't easily fit inside your pack, you can sandwich it between the lid and the pack body or clip it to the outside bottom of your pack.

Chapter Ten

Summary of Hikes, Planning Timeline, and Packing Checklist

SUMMARY OF HIKES

	Nootka	North Coast & Cape Scott Trail	Tatchu	West Coast Trail
Trail type	One-way	One-way	Out and back	One way
Length of trail	36 km (22.4 miles)	60 km (37 miles)	64 km (40 miles)	75 km (47 miles)
# Days needed	4-6	5-7	5-7	5-8
Reservation needed?	no	no	no	Yes www.reservation.pc.gc.ca

BACKPACKING VANCOUVER ISLAND 101

	Nootka	North Coast & Cape Scott Trail	Tatchu	West Coast Trail
Hiking fees	$20 group landing fee. $50/ adult, payable to Mowachaht/ Muchalaht First Nation in cash, in person, or online. https://explorenootka.com/pf/hiking/	$10/ night. Payable online to BC parks: https://camping.bcparks.ca/, or pay with cash at trailhead	n/a	$300-420 per person *Trail permit *Reservation fee *Ferry fee *National Park entry fee
Closest airport	Nanaimo (YCD)	Port Hardy (YZT)	Nanaimo (YCD)	*Nanaimo (YCD) *Victoria (YYJ)
Trail access points	*Tahsis *Zeballos *Gold River	Port Hardy	*Tahsis *Zeballos *Gold River	*Bamfield *Nitinat *Port Renfrew
Trailheads	*Yuquot (Friendly Cove) *Louie Bay Lagoon *Louie Bay (Tongue Point)	*Shushartie Bay *Cape Scott Parking Lot	*Yellow Bluff Bay *Rugged Point	*Bamfield (Pacheena Bay Campground) *Nitinat (Nitinat Lake Recreational Site) *Port Renfrew (Gordon River/ Pacheedaht Campground)
Trailhead access	Water taxi with Shorebird Expeditions: https://shorebirdexpeditions.com/expeditions/hike-nootka-sound/ or Zeballos Expeditions: https://www.zeballosexpeditions.com/transportation.html Float plane with Air Nootka: https://www.airnootka.com/hiking)	Water taxi and shuttle with Cape Scott Water Taxi & North Coast Trail Shuttle: https://www.capescottwatertaxi.ca/	Water taxi with Shorebird Expeditions: https://shorebirdexpeditions.com/expeditions/hike-nootka-sound/ or Zeballos Expeditions: https://www.zeballosexpeditions.com/transportation.html Float plane with Air Nootka: https://www.airnootka.com/hiking)	*Car *Bus to/ between all three trailheads (Gordon River, Nitinat, and Pachena Bay) https://trailbus.com/
Tidal station	Saavedra Islands (08645)	Cape Scott (08790)	Kyuquot (08710)	Tofino (08615)
Outhouses	X	✓	X	✓
Bear caches	X	✓	X	✓

PLANNING TIMELINE

Up to 8 months before hike
- ☐ Gather your hiking crew
- ☐ Choose your hike
- ☐ Choose your hiking dates
- ☐ Reserve your spot on the trail and pay for permits and/ or trail fees

3-6 months before hike
- ☐ Arrange transportation
  - ☐ To Vancouver Island (ferry, plane)
  - ☐ To the trail access point (car, bus)
  - ☐ To the trailhead (water taxi, seaplane, bus)
- ☐ Arrange overnight stay at trail access point (h/motel, AirBnB, hostel, campsite)
- ☐ Physical training

3 months before hike
- ☐ Take inventory of your gear and food
- ☐ Buy map, gear and food

1-2 months before hike
- ☐ Practice overnight hikes
- ☐ Map your itinerary

1-2 weeks before hike
- ☐ Pack your backpack

BACKPACKING VANCOUVER ISLAND 101

PACKING CHECKLIST

Hiking
- ☐ Hiking bottoms
- ☐ Hiking shirt
- ☐ Sports bra
- ☐ Underwear
- ☐ Wool socks
- ☐ Hiking shoes
- ☐ Backpack (+ rain cover)
- ☐ Poles
- ☐ Gaiters
- ☐ Bear spray & holster
- ☐ Sunglasses
- ☐ Sun hat
- ☐ Waterproof phone/ camera case with lanyard
- ☐ Waterproof map & tide table
- ☐ Fanny pack

Water
- ☐ Water container(s)
- ☐ Filtration/ purification

Shelter/ sleeping
- ☐ Tent
- ☐ Tent footprint
- ☐ Tarp
- ☐ Ground mat
- ☐ Pillow
- ☐ Eye mask
- ☐ Ear plugs
- ☐ Sleeping bag → in a dry compression bag

Clothes → in a dry compression bag (and no cotton!)
- ☐ Thermal top/ fleece
- ☐ Thermal pants
- ☐ Socks (2 pairs for hiking, 1 thick pair for camp, 1 extra)
- ☐ Down jacket
- ☐ Toque/ beanie
- ☐ Gloves
- ☐ Camp shoes/ sandals
- ☐ Rain jacket & pants
- ☐ Water shoes
- ☐ Second hiking shirt
- ☐ Camp pants/ shorts

Kitchen
- ☐ Stove
- ☐ Fuel
- ☐ Lighter
- ☐ Pot
- ☐ Bowl
- ☐ Cup
- ☐ Utensil
- ☐ Biodegradable soap
- ☐ Aeropress & filters

Food → in a dry bag
- ☐ ___Breakfasts
- ☐ ___Lunches
- ☐ ___Snacks
- ☐ ___Dinner
- ☐ ___Treats
- ☐ ___Drinks

Toiletries
- ☐ Toothbrush
- ☐ Toothpaste
- ☐ Floss
- ☐ Deodorant
- ☐ Hair brush & elastics
- ☐ Lotion
- ☐ Sunscreen
- ☐ Insect repellant
- ☐ Feminine hygiene products
- ☐ Biodegradable toilet paper (1-2 rolls)
- ☐ Biodegradable wipes
- ☐ Sanitizer
- ☐ Medication

DOMINIQUE LEVESQUE

Gear
- ☐ GPS receiver
- ☐ Rope/ paracord
- ☐ Carabiners (1 locking)
- ☐ Tarp (with pegs and straps/ rope)
- ☐ Headlamp & batteries
- ☐ Battery pack
- ☐ Knife/ leatherman

Emergency/ first aid
- ☐ Whistle
- ☐ Emergency blanket
- ☐ Knife
- ☐ Compass
- ☐ Mirror
- ☐ Fire starter
- ☐ Lighter
- ☐ Tea light candles
- ☐ Water purification tablets
- ☐ Bandages
- ☐ Blister care
- ☐ Tweezers
- ☐ Tape (climber's tape, electrical tape)
- ☐ Gear repair kit
- ☐ Zip ties
- ☐ Extra batteries

Miscellaneous
- ☐ Trowel
- ☐ Towel
- ☐ Chair/ foam knee pad
- ☐ Day pack
- ☐ Speaker
- ☐ Musical instrument
- ☐ Fairy lights
- ☐ Hand warmers
- ☐ Cash
- ☐ Extra ziplock bags/ plastic bags

Other
- ☐
- ☐
- ☐
- ☐
- ☐

Chapter Eleven

Conclusion

Well, folks, there you have it – a thorough guidebook to get you hiking, enjoying nature, and exploring the coast of Vancouver Island. After learning about safety in the wild, how to plan your travels, how to map your hiking itinerary, and what you will need to pack, I trust that you now feel unstoppably confident to take on a multi-day hiking adventure in this part of the world. Perhaps the last piece is to go practice! The more overnight/ thru-hikes you complete, the more confident and at ease you will feel in the outback. One last pro tip:

PRO TIP: When drying your hiking boots by the fire at night, put hot stones inside them and they will dry faster!

Thank you for inviting me along your journey of preparation and wilderness exploration. I wish you the best of luck out there and in your future nature endeavours! You got this!

If you've enjoyed reading this guidebook, please take a moment to provide a favourable review on Amazon; I'd very much appreciate it!

Resources and References

Brown, A. (2024, April 24). *How to pack a backpack*. MSR The Summit Register. https://www.msrgear.com/blog/how-to-pack-a-backpack/.

Contributor, F. (2023, July 31). *The 10 Toughest/Most Dangerous Treks in the World*. MapQuest Travel. https://www.mapquest.com/travel/the-10-toughestmost-dangerous-treks-in-the-world/.

Explore Nootka (2024). *Nootka Trail Weekly Hiking Pass*. Explore Nootka. https://explorenootka.com/product/nootka-trail-weekly-hiking-pass/

Explore Nootka. (2024). *Yuquot Heritage Site Landing Fee*. Explore Nootka. https://explorenootka.com/product/yuquot-heritage-site-landing-fee/

Garay, E. (2024). *What to wear hiking*. Recreational Equipment Inc. https://www.rei.com/learn/expert-advice/how-to-choose-hiking-clothes.html#Hiking_Accessories

Government of Canada. (2024, July 3). *Cape Scott (08790)*. https://www.tides.gc.ca/en/stations/08790.

Hansen, D. (2013, March 19). *Hanging a Bear Bag—The PCT method – the ultimate hang*. https://theultimatehang.com/2013/03/19/hanging-a-bear-bag-the-pct-method/.

Leave No Trace. (2023, September 6). *The 7 Principles - Leave No Trace Center for Outdoor Ethics*. https://lnt.org/why/7-principles/.

Ministry of Environment and Climate Change Strategy. (2022, February 2). *Staying safe around wildlife*. Province of British Columbia. https://www2.gov.bc.ca/gov/content/environment/plants-animals-ecosystems/wildlife/human-wildlife-conflict/staying-safe-around-wildlife.

Parks Canada Agency, Government of Canada. (2024, August 28). *West Coast Trail: Hike of a lifetime*. Pacific Rim National Park Reserve. https://parks.canada.ca/pn-np/bc/pacificrim/activ/sco-wct.

REI Co-op. (2024). *Backpacking Food Ideas & Meal Planning*. Recreational Equipment Inc. https://www.rei.com/learn/expert-advice/planning-menu.html.

REI Co-op. (2024). *How to Choose a Backpack*. Recreational Equipment Inc. https://www.rei.com/learn/expert-advice/backpack.html.

REI Co-op. (2024). *How to Choose a Water Filter or Purifier*. Recreational Equipment Inc. https://www.rei.com/learn/expert-advice/water-treatment-backcountry.html.

REI Co-op. (2024). *How to Choose and Use a GPS*. Recreational Equipment Inc. https://www.rei.com/learn/expert-advice/gps-receiver.html#:~:text=Once%20revolutionary%2C%20GPS%20technology%20is,where%20you%20want%20to%20go.

REI Co-op. (2024). *How to Use a Compass*. Recreational Equipment Inc. https://www.rei.com/learn/expert-advice/navigation-basics.html.

Tilton, B. (2006). *Outdoor safety handbook*. Stackpole Books.